Praise for *Church Fights*

"*Church Fights* is raw, real, and redemptive. Jamie Centeno pulls no punches in sharing his journey from pain to purpose, rebellion to revival. This book is a prophetic wake-up call to the Church—a challenge to trade performance for presence, popularity for purity, and compromise for consecration. Jamie's story will stir your spirit, break your heart, and reignite your passion for God's house. Every pastor, church leader, and believer needs to read this."

Samuel Rodriguez, Lead Pastor, New Season Church, President, National Hispanic Christian Leadership Conference

—⁓—

"Thoughtful words brilliantly written. The clarity will draw you in. You will find it hard to put down this book. Jamie Centeno has the heart of a pastor and parent while bringing healing to the soul. Thank you, Jamie for writing *Church Fights*. I recommend it to all my friends."

Bishop Michael Pitts, Cornerstone Global Network

"In *Church Fights* Apostle Jamie Centeno declares war on compromise and complacency. With wisdom and compassion, he calls us forward through this page turner. Apostle Jamie is full of transparency and truth; he is honest and honorable. Apostle Jamie as a battle tested true spiritual father and general is willing to share his pain and show his scars so that we might learn from his mistakes. Shame hides, but loves shares. He graciously and generously shares his pain for our gain and God's glory.

"The mark of a true spiritual father is someone who is willing to be transparent and vulnerable and admit their mistakes to save others from unnecessary pain. Apostle Jamie does this because he cares more about the people than how the people perceive him. *Church Fights* smashes idols and soothes the soul. It's a true invitation to repent, reprioritize and return to our first love by putting Christ first in everything once again."

Pastor Adam LiVecchi, Founder of We See Jesus Ministries and Senior Pastor of Rescue Church in West New York, New Jersey, Author of *Go. Preach. Heal, Listen. Learn. Obey, Follow. Lead. Mentor* and *7 Keys to Success*

—✦—

"Jamie Centeno is the real deal. With honesty and conviction, he shares the compelling testimony of how God called him "out of darkness into His marvelous light" (1 Peter 2:9). This is a story of personal revival—a life transformed by God's grace and the Holy Spirit's power—which, in turn, is sparking corporate revival and transformation in the lives of many. I highly recommend this book because I believe you will be challenged, encouraged, and strengthened by each page that you read."

Dr. Ché Ahn, Senior Leader, Harvest Rock Church, Pasadena, CA, President, Harvest International Ministry, International Chancellor, Wagner University

—✦—

"*Church Fights* conveys a timely message. My friend Jamie Centeno writes with deep conviction and anointed eloquence. What he shares comes from real experience and calls the Church back to purity, back to focus, and back to the presence of God. In a time of noise, this work clearly communicates a direct message. I believe the Lord will use this book to awaken many to the deeper things of the Spirit."

David Diga Hernandez, Evangelist, Author

"This inspiring and prophetic book reminds us of the Lord's example—how Christ loved the church and gave His life for it. Despite its imperfections, the church remains God's chosen vehicle to transform lives, connect hearts, and impact our communities. Apostle Jamie Centeno challenges us to prioritize the presence of God above all else, exposing the dangers of entertainment-driven Christianity and compromise. It urges believers to seek the true fire of the Spirit and to love the church with divine passion. A must-read for anyone longing to see the church restored in power, holiness, and as the bride of Christ. This book will stir your heart, convict your spirit, and realign you with the divine purpose of loving and advancing the church for this generation."

Omar Lopez, Lead Pastor of Reach Network

"In my fifty-three years of being born again and raised up in a dynamic Spirit-filled church, I've seen and heard a lot of descriptions of the bride of Christ called the Ecclesia. Being saved in what's been called the "Jesus Movement," and experiencing in my local church an outpouring of God's presence with my friend Tommy Tenny (author of *God Chasers*) for three and a half years, I can tell you this bride is maturing and getting rid of a lot of spots and wrinkles. She's turning into a Glorious Church! My friend Jamie, through his well-defined journey, has turned into a worshipping warrior. I admit, I love a good fight! I grew up with a father that was a Golden Gloves boxer in the army. He taught me to box and how to dance, bob and weave, and keep from getting beat! This book is for winners, fighters, and worshipping warriors not wimps. Read it and live it, and you'll win Him!"

Bishop Bart Pierce, Founder Rock City Church, Baltimore, MD

—◦◊◦—

"Pastor Jamie has distinguished himself as a leader of leaders. His pastoral style and influence in Philadelphia have defined him as out of the box. In *Church Fights* he gives us a glimpse of the man, his formation and the contributions, which have helped to form him as an apostle, pastor, and peer to so many. Those who know him, find his genuine and practical approach to faith in Christ refreshing."

Phil Hernandez, Founder of In The Light Ministries

—∞—

"When you grow up in church, you meet church before you meet God. That was Pastor Jamie. He knew church, knew how to do it all, but he still had to meet God for himself. And once he did, the real *fight* started. Stepping into ministry, starting a church, and facing every kind of battle you can imagine, *Church Fights* tells that story. It's not polished, and that's what makes it powerful. It's honest. It's messy. It's ministry. Showing what it looks like when God's grace shows up in the middle of the fight. If you've ever been wounded in church, questioned your calling, or thought about quitting, read this. God still calls. He still speaks. And He still uses people like us."

Apostle Kelly Lohrke, Pastor, Church Planter and President of The Cure Church Network

—∞—

"In *Church Fights*, Jamie Centeno delivers a powerful message on the current state of the contemporary church, challenging the status quo and calling for a return to the core structure of faith and the gospel. With transparent and truthful conviction, Jamie shares his journey as a pastor's kid navigating the challenges and complexities of identity, community, and spirituality.

"Jamie's personal experiences and biblical truths, stir up a sense of urgency for authentic encounters with God, as he urges readers to prioritize the presence of God while warning against the pitfalls of worldly acceptance and complacency. *Church Fights* is more than a book; it's a timely reminder that the church is a transformative force. It's a call for revival and authenticity within the body of Christ. In this book, Jamie challenges readers to confront the modern church culture, prioritize presence over programs, and fight for the legacy of faith and the gospel that will ignite future generations. If you want to know what it truly means to be a part of a living, breathing church that reflects the heart of God, then this book is for you!"

Pastor Reina Olmeda, Director of Mental Health Initiative, National Hispanic Christian Leadership Conference, Pastor, Transformation Church LV, Author, *Fit For Your Assignments*

—◊◊◊—

"Reading *Church Fights* moved me deeply. It is more than one man's story. Rather, it is the story of many who have wrestled with hurt, shame, and misunderstanding within the Church. Yet page after page, you witness God's grace breaking through, leading to healing, humility, and hope. This book is a gift to the body of Christ, showing us that the only true victory is found in yielding to the love of our gracious King, Jesus Christ, and desperately pursuing His presence."

Pastor Terry M. Davis, Executive Director, Philadelphia Gospel Movement

———❧———

"In *Church Fights*, Jamie Centeno offered me an opportunity to do what every veteran youth pastor should have the opportunity to do at some point in their life—see life through the eyes of the students that they poured their lives into. I lived through Rounds 1-5 of this book as the Youth Pastor leading the Youth Ministry that Jamie so aptly describes fighting against. I read the stories in those chapters and remember it all as if it were yesterday. It is a surreal thing to look at memories of one's life through the eyes of another. As one who had an up-front seat for Rounds 1-5, I bore many a bruise from the lashing out of Jamie's early fight against the world, the church, his family and his faith. Now, more than thirty years later, because of that lived experience of the disorientation and pain of Rounds 1-5, I find myself incredibly encouraged and inspired by the transformation and insight flowing out of the pages in the following eight rounds of the story.

"It has been repeated often that "pain not transformed is pain transmitted." It is a gift to read how Gospel freedom transformed Jamie's life from the bondage of transmitted pain into a new reality where wounds became wombs birthing seeds of restoration and renewal. That's a reality worth fighting for. I praise God for the way He passionately fought for Jamie, choosing never to surrender or back down. The story in *Church Fights* is a testimony to a life surrendered to the Gold Medal Fighter who fought on our behalf and won. Read *Church Fights* if you want to learn how to live and love in the light of that marvelous truth."

Joel Van Dyke, D.Min., Pastor, Lee St. Church, Wyoming, MI, Senior Fellow, Street Psalms, Founder: Centro para la Mision

Churchs
Fights

Confronting the
Enemies of the Church

Jamie Centeno

ILLUMIFY
MEDIA.COM

Church Fights

Published by
Illumify Media Global
www.IllumifyMedia.com
"Let's bring your book to life!"

Church Fights
www.jamiecenteno.net
Email: admin@ilight.tv

Give feedback on the book at: feedback@ilight.tv

First Edition: 2025

Paperback ISBN: 978-1-964251-78-3

Cover design by Debbie Lewis

Printed in the United States of America

To all the Kingdom of heaven pioneers who were meet with resistance when all they wanted to do was make a difference in the city of Philadelphia. If you were knock down and didn't stop fighting this book is for you.

Contents

Prologue

Let's be honest. Somewhere along the way, the church seems to have lost its power. We've become polished, professional, and popular, but we lack the punch of the Spirit. We've got lights but not much fire. We've got followers, but very few have picked up their cross. There's a growing surge of carnality creeping in, and it's no longer hiding in the back row. It's on the worship team, leading small groups, and teaching the kids. We are producing crowds who know how to sing the right lyrics but don't carry the right lifestyle. Unchanged, unfazed, and unmoved, many attend weekly but haven't truly encountered God.

This generation—especially our young people—is in an identity crisis of epic proportions. Confusion is reigning while conviction is retreating. The world is moving at a hellish speed, and the Church is choking on its dust. Darkness has been accelerating while many in the Church are decelerating. Our youth's attention is captured more by TikTok than by truth. And we wonder why they are struggling to know who they are. The issue isn't just "out there"; it's in our pews, in our pulpits, and in our playlists. We're becoming watered-down, world-friendly, entertainment-driven institutions that fear offending people more than we fear grieving the Holy Spirit.

Jesus is coming back. That's not just good theology; it's divine reality. And Scripture gives us sobering warnings: goats and sheep, wheat and chaff, one taken and one left. Narrow is the road that leads to life, and few find it—not because it's hidden, but because it's costly. It requires discipline, devotion, and a desire to be holy. While some metaphors in Scripture are layered and symbolic, many signs are crystal clear: Wars and rumors of wars. Families betraying one another. Signs in the heavens. These aren't vague hints; they are flashing indicators of a soon-coming King.

What kind of church will Jesus return to find? Will we resemble the Laodicean church in Revelation—lukewarm, self-sufficient, and unaware of our spiritual poverty? As a pastor, I've visited many churches—beautiful buildings, polished worship, dynamic kids' ministries. I've sat in the seats and thought, "Man, I wish our sound system was this good" or "If only our children's ministry was on this level." But then, as the music plays and the lights dim, I find myself disoriented. Because while it all sounds good... where is God?

I'm watching the stage, but I'm not beholding the throne. I leave entertained but not transformed. I'm told that all is good but not compelled to seek Jesus. Shouldn't the presence of God leave me weeping with awe, hungry for the Word, and wrecked with holy conviction? Is the anointing something we still contend for, or is it just a nostalgic idea from a bygone era?

Today, churches are going viral for scandals, not sanctification. We're known more for our controversies than our consecration. Our sermons are digestible, our music is culturally approved, and the world has started applauding us. But here's the catch: when we are most accepted by the world, we are often least aligned with the Spirit. We started walking in their circles, then found ourselves standing in their approval, and eventually sitting comfortably at their tables. Now, anyone who dares to challenge us gets labeled a "hater" or dismissed as a "religious Pharisee." It's the very progression Psalm 1 warns us about—walking with the ungodly, standing in their way, and finally sitting in the seat of the scornful.

Listen, I love when church can be cool. But if our coolness has made us lukewarm, count me out. I'd rather have fire than flair. I'm not trying to sound like an extremist, but I've met too many insecure pastors chasing what they think they lack instead of pressing into what truly matters. And the danger? We start chasing the stuff—sound systems, casual styles, coffee bars—first while forgetting the one thing we were called to pursue, such as the presence of God.

The weighty Shechinah of His presence is worth its weight in gold. This would cultivate a deep reverence and hunger to know God more intimately. Without it, we're just a social club with a playlist. We've made strides in excellence, but we've also made compromises in reverence. We've built churches that appeal to audiences, but do they host the Almighty?

If the authority of the Church is going to be restored, we must be ready for the persecution, resistance, and rejection that comes with it. Jesus told us plainly that the world will hate us if we truly follow Him. In John 15:18–19 it says, "If the world hates you, you know that it hated Me before it hated you. If you were of the world, the world would love its own. Yet because you are not of the world, but I chose you out of the world, therefore the world hates you." Jesus made it clear—if we truly follow Him, we shouldn't be surprised when the world turns against us. The souls of men are at stake. Where they spend hinges on whether we choose popularity or presence. The blood of this generation is on our hands if we trade truth for applause.

My prayer is that this book will serve as a prophetic call to take up arms to some and a divine confirmation to others. May it stir us, convict us, and realign us with our true calling. Because make no mistake the soul of the United States of America is tethered to the soul of the Church. And the soul of the Church must be anchored in the presence of God. That's the only thing worth fighting for.

PASTOR'S KID
vs
CHURCH

Round 1 | The Weigh-In

It feels strange trying to trace things back to the beginning. There's nothing particularly cinematic about how my life started. I wasn't born with a halo or a dramatic prophetic word. I was just another Puerto Rican kid from North Philadelphia—one of thousands stacked into row homes and raised on rice, red Kool-Aid, and the soundtrack of sirens and salsa. Survival wasn't a struggle; it was just the norm.

In 1983, when I was eight years old, we lived in a house on Dauphin Street near Fifth. It was the kind of place where you knew the neighbors, not because of community meetings but because the walls were too thin to ignore their fights. The corner bodega was owned by Asians, and directly across the street was Sanchez's Bar. Philly street parties weren't city-approved. They were hydrants cracked open in the summer heat, *pinchos* (kabobs) sizzling on a well-worn grill, and boom boxes giving birth to the next block anthem.

We didn't have lush green parks. We had grey cracked pavements. Our playground was a two-block radius in every direction. We played manhunt in alleyways and ducked behind rusted cars. We climbed fences, jumped roofs, and dared each other to explore abandoned fire-charred houses with floors that creaked like they were ready to collapse, which they usually did. We flirted with danger not because we were brave, but because we were bored.

But that was normal. That was North Philly normal.

What wasn't so typical was the size of our family. At the time, I was one of six kids—four brothers and a sister (another sister would be born later). I fell smack dab in the middle, of the boys, at least. However, as the only girl (at the time) my sister's status gave her a unique placement in the sibling hierarchy. My middle-child syndrome didn't come with a therapist's diagnosis. It was baptized in noise, clutter, hand-me-downs, and the constant hustle for attention.

We had something else many didn't: a mom and a dad who were married. And not just married, but mission minded. My dad wasn't a banker or a mechanic; he was a street evangelist and urban missionary, the first one in his family to be radically saved by Jesus. He carried this holy burden to preach in every crack and crevice of the city. He might not have had much money, but he had a mission from God.

One of the coolest things he ever did was build us a wooden fort in the backyard. That might not sound like much today, but back then? It was a fortress, a pirate ship, a castle—whatever we needed it to be. Our yard became the envy of the neighborhood. I'm pretty sure he built that fort to keep us close and to give us something to belong to when the streets tried to offer something more seductive.

Looking back, I see it more clearly now: I was always fighting. Fighting to understand where I belonged.

Maybe it was a middle child thing, but I felt like I lived in the in-between. I was too light skinned to be fully Puerto Rican and too Puerto Rican to be considered white. I didn't speak Spanish, but I devoured *arroz con gandules* (Puerto Rican Rice with Pigeon Peas), loved Abuela's café con leche, and was accustomed in *familia* culture where everyone is in everyone's business.

I was churched up on Sunday mornings—Sunday school, youth group and joining in on family Bible studies—but when I had time during the week, I was running the streets with friends who came from broken homes, with moms strung out on the couch and older siblings caught up in gangs.

I was caught in-between denominations too. My dad raised missionary support from white Presbyterian churches and black Mennonite fellowships while we attended a Spanish Baptist church. My Sunday worship experiences were as diverse as the Philadelphia Zoo.

And school? That was another layer of the identity crisis. I went from a rough inner-city school in Philly, one with mostly black and brown kids (and a very generous grading curve), to a predominantly white Christian school in the suburbs of Lansdale, Pennsylvania, one with actual academic expectations. I survived, somehow. But the culture shock was real.

Even my name—Jamie—kept me suspended in ambiguity. Boy or girl? Latino or white? Street kid or church boy? I didn't know who I was, and it made me feel like I belonged nowhere. I was always in the middle.

That fight for identity, for clarity, for belonging didn't manifest as toughness. No, I wasn't some street-hardened warrior. I was a scared kid in a confusing world. And I fought it—not with fists, but with foolishness.

I fought for attention in the streets by breaking windshields and throwing rocks at cars. I fought for identity in classrooms by becoming the clown, the disruptor, the one who made people laugh, so they wouldn't look too closely. I fought at home by shutting down at dinner or making slick comments when my dad called us for family devotions. He'd try to sit us down to read the Bible and share God's heart, and I'd roll my eyes, cross my arms, and resist every holy word. Not because I didn't love him, but because I didn't understand why I was supposed to love everything he stood for.

What people in the church didn't see was the other fight, the invisible one. The night terrors that had me sleepwalking in fear. The pornographic images that snuck into my imagination and poisoned the innocence I hadn't yet learned to protect. The sadness I carried in my chest. The feeling that I was never enough—not for my dad, not for the church, not for God.

I wasn't out here trying to be a villain. I just didn't know how to be the hero they were expecting me to be. So I rebelled. Not because I wanted to break rules,

7

but because I didn't know how to live under so many of them. And, yes, there were spankings. My dad had the infamous "spanking stick" and wasn't afraid to use it. My school had its own system of discipline too. I earned detentions like badges of dishonor. Got expelled once, maybe twice. I even took a whupping from the principal, and I remember thinking, "This is lightweight compared to my dad." It almost gave me a sick sense of pride. Like I had a pain tolerance the other kids couldn't match.

Meanwhile, my parents were fighting battles bigger than me. Fighting for other people's marriages. Fighting addiction in other families. Fighting poverty in our own. And in the middle of that, there I was, mouthing off, slamming doors, and finding ways to secretly do whatever I wanted.

I'm sure my siblings had their own issues that kept my parents on their toes, but I know for a fact I kept my parents on their knees. I was their full-time prayer request. I was the kid they whispered about after church, the one who made people say, "Isn't that the pastor's son?"

Yes. Yes, I was.

For a long time, that title didn't feel like a calling. It felt like a cage.

But they didn't give up. They fought for me. On their knees. In intercession. With tears and trembling. And let me tell you, they won.

It would take years of wandering, failing, resisting, rebelling. But the seeds they planted, the prayers they prayed, the discipline they gave, it all worked. Eventually.

And that's where this story starts—not with a highlight reel, but with the reality of a boy caught in the middle of everything, slowly learning how to fight the bad things in the right way. And learning who was fighting for him all along.

Round 2 | Toe to Toe

There I was, standing in the back of my father's church, hands up, squaring off with a guy from the youth group. We had just come back from an overnight camp where everyone was hyped up on Jesus and making fresh commitments to live for God. Apparently, none of us took in the part about loving your enemies, because that was the last thing we were doing in that moment. The youth group had gathered around us like it was an episode of *Fight Club: Youth Group Edition.*

Now, let me be clear. I was no thug. I may have fantasized about being Bruce Lee, but at thirteen years old I wasn't about to throw out any untested kung fu moves. I knew my lane: wrestling. So I grabbed this boy, lifted him clean off the ground, and held him there as he punched me on the top of my head. I didn't slam him, just set him back down. He stepped back, probably shocked I was strong enough to even do that.

This all started at camp. Word got around that he had it out for me. I didn't even know why. He wasn't a church kid; he was from the streets and had been invited to camp because he "needed Jesus." Instead, he had his sights set on crucifying me. Leaders tried to talk to us, but he wasn't interested in peace. I spent the whole retreat watching my back.

As soon as we pulled up to the church in Philly, he was ready to throw hands. Of all places, this fight was about to go down behind the church—my father's church. I looked around and saw that none of my "friends" had my back. That hurt more than anything. But then I spotted one of the older guys, a street guy connected to the church, who came to pick up his little sister. I told him what was happening, and he promised to keep it fair. He even checked the guy for weapons.

We went behind the church. The crowd formed. The fight broke out. It was maybe five minutes, but it felt like a lifetime. Eventually, one of the youth leaders rounded the corner and broke it up. People scattered. I was relieved. I remember thinking, "Thank God, I'm saved."

Then came the sit-down. Me, my dad, and the guy who just threatened my life. My dad, trying to play peacemaker, asked for a truce. I said I had no problem with the guy. Then right in front of my father, the boy says, "This isn't over until one of us can't get up." I looked at my dad, expecting him to put this guy in his place. But all he said was something like, "I'm sorry to hear that. I wish we could've worked it out."

I felt totally abandoned, not just by my friends but by my own father, the pastor of the church. I wasn't just physically alone in the fight; I was emotionally alone. And church? Church didn't feel safe anymore. I concluded that day that church made men weak.

Oh, and did I mention the guy lived across the street from the church? Right next to the youth center. My head would have to be on a swivel every time I left the building.

As a pastor's kid, I already had tension with the church. I didn't always want to go, but I had started to accept it and even made some friends and enjoyed some perks. But after that fight, all of it shattered. I felt humiliated. I felt like I didn't matter. And that's when rejection took a deeper root in my soul.

I couldn't tell you the exact age that spirit of rejection entered, but this was one of the key moments it tightened its grip. I became angry and started acting out. I battled depression, and it came out in how I treated others. I took it out on people in the church. People who were weaker than me, or just different. I'd make mean, sarcastic comments that made others laugh. One of those people was a young girl who showed up looking for her little brother. I was brutal. The youth leaders were furious. She almost didn't come back. I'm grateful she did because today she's my wife.

The executive pastor's son worked for my dad, and all I saw in him was someone weak and naïve, a wannabe. I made him pay. It's not who I wanted to be, but something about being at church flipped a switch. We even messed with guys in the church's rehab program—guys who were trying to get their lives right. I was messed up.

In church services, I'd sit in the back with a bad attitude. I mocked people, mocked worship, mocked handicaps. I used my words like weapons, verbal Jiu Jitsu. Sarcasm became my go-to defense and offense. I was a menace in youth group. I hurt a lot of people who came looking for love but found only my pain instead.

There was this one moment with my dad that's still burned into my memory. We were in the car, just the two of us, and I had done something—who knows what, there was always something—and he was giving me one of his classic lectures: long, intense, serious voice, full of Scripture, disappointment, and moral weight. He was talking nonstop, and I just sat there getting more and more angry. Every word felt like a shovel digging deeper the pit of failure I already lived in.

He didn't let me talk. I wasn't even allowed to respond. So I just started arguing with him in my head. Line for line, I had a comeback, a defense, a reason, a cry for understanding, but none of it came out. Instead, I stayed quiet and let my imagination fight the battle for me.

Then he dropped the spiritual hammer on me: "Children, obey your parents in the Lord, for this is right."

Without thinking—without skipping a beat—I shot back: "Doesn't it also say, 'Fathers, don't exasperate your children?'"

Silence. I didn't even know how I knew that verse. I had never rehearsed it or studied it for a moment like that. But it came flying out of my mouth like a flaming arrow. He was stunned. I was stunned. We both just sat in it.

I didn't say it as a humble Bible student. I said it as a son who felt like he was drowning and finally found a Scripture that screamed, "You're pushing me too far."

To this day, youth leaders tell me how much they despised me. And I get it. Today, I playfully say, "Y'all need Jesus if you can't forgive that knucklehead from thirty years ago," but I understand. I was toxic.

In the middle of all that chaos, my best friend helped spark a music group called One Way. It was drama, rap, testimonies—a whole creative ministry. I wasn't saved, but I knew how to blend in. I knew how to be "churchy." I even started rapping.

One time, after being punished for something dumb I did, I was so angry with my dad that I wrote a rap. It was inspired by Fresh Prince's "Parents Just Don't Understand," but mine was about the struggle of being a pastor's kid. I wanted to perform it on testimony night—drop a lyrical bomb in front of the church.

Instead, the group One Way gave me a beat, and I reworked the song. That song became something I performed for years. It was my therapy. A venting session in rhyme. A pastor's kid's beef with the church. But before I go too far, let me set the scene.

I used to think our family was way too big—seven of us packed into a row home, coming out of vehicles like a clown's magic trick. Just when I thought we couldn't possibly add one more, my youngest sister (the seventh child) came along, the latest addition to our not-so-little tribe. It was loud, it was layered, and it was full of life… and drama.

Looking back, I was bitter and broken. I was angry with the God of my father and took it out on the church of my father. But God had more grace for me than I deserved. Sure, I had moments where I was kind, friendly, and even loving. But for the most part, it was darkness.

Despite my behavior, the church was doing good. It was creative, outward focused. It served the community. It gave young people opportunities to express themselves. It brought together people from all walks of life.

It gave people hope.

But I couldn't see that back then. Not from the pit I was in. All I saw was a church that felt more like my father's mistress than the bride of Christ. It stole his time, his attention, and in my eyes his loyalty. I didn't understand how something that was supposed to be holy could leave me feeling so wounded, alone, and forgotten. God felt like a distant concept, not a present Father. Jesus was more like a Sunday school story than a Savior. And without even realizing it, I was becoming a weapon in the enemy's hands, being used to lash out against the very thing that had the power to set my heart free.

It took years for the truth to unravel in my spirit. I wasn't really fighting my dad. I wasn't even fighting the church. I was fighting a spirit of religion that had invaded a sacred space. The church didn't hurt me—religion did. Religion is what makes people fake strong and secretly weak. It's what hands out rules without relationship. Religion replaces sacred encounters with empty programs, where we trade transformation for behavior management.

Jesus was building His church the whole time, but our human fingerprints distorted the view. We substituted God's presence for polished performance. And I mistook the pain of that distortion as the failure of the church itself.

Back then, I was blind to all of that. And unfortunately, things would get darker before I ever saw the light.

Round 3 | No Mas

The moonlight felt eerie as it crept into my room on the third floor of our packed house. Even though the place was full—my mom and dad, brothers and sisters, and even a single mom and her daughter we had taken in—I felt completely alone in the universe.

The voices were getting louder.

"It would be better if I didn't exist."

"My life is so sad."

"You hurt so many people."

"The pain would go away in death."

Despite the therapy, despite the meds for insomnia, things were getting worse. I was suicidal. I didn't want to live.

Every night the thoughts came back, but this night—this night I couldn't stand it anymore.

It was 1992. I was seventeen now, and a few weeks before, the one girl I had opened my heart to—the one I thought I'd marry—ended it. We had been together for over three years. We had been youth group sweethearts. She was my best friend, my confidant, my identity. I was faithful and true, but I was also obsessive. She had become my world, and everything else faded into the background. God, church, family, school, none of it mattered compared to her.

Eventually, I became too much. She wanted to grow in her relationship with God, and a youth leader encouraged her to break it off with me. So she did. At church. With that leader there to make sure she followed through.

She looked at me with sadness, not anger. She wasn't pushing me away because of something I had done, but because she wanted more of God. And I was in the way.

I ugly cried. I pleaded. I begged. But she stood her ground. The youth leader eventually stepped in and held me back as she left the room. I collapsed, broken.

"Why would God take her away?"

"Why would He hurt me like this?"

That night I ran away to a friend's house. I didn't want to be home. I didn't want to be anywhere.

The next day, I walked into my dad's office at church and told him everything. To my surprise, he didn't scold me. He didn't go into full pastor mode. He just listened. He comforted me. For the first time in a long time, I felt seen by him.

But the relief didn't last.

I went back to school, but I was in a daze. I sat through youth group like a ghost. I wrote dark poetry in my journal. I told my therapist what I could. I tried listening to worship music just to keep from drowning, but everything felt like a Band-Aid on a bullet wound.

The depression stuck to me like a shadow. And over time, it started to feel, well, comfortable, safe even. It was my companion.

That's when the voices got bolder.

Invisible assailants whispered in the dark.

"You're a disappointment as a son."

"You've failed as a brother."

"You're not even a good friend."

"You're stupid."

"Untalented."

"Ugly."

"Unlovable."

"If even she doesn't love you, why stay?"

I was tired of fighting. Tired of trying to be understood. Tired of being unloved.

I walked to the medicine cabinet and stared at the warning label on the sleeping pills.

"It's that easy."

"They'll finally care."

"It won't hurt."

I was warring with the temptation to unalive myself. I knew this wasn't right. I walked back to my bed. The voices didn't stop, so I got up again. This time, instead of reaching for the pills, I crumbled to my knees by a chair in my room.

And I prayed.

It wasn't pretty. It wasn't poetic. It was raw.

"God... if you're real... the God my parents serve... I need You. I'm suffering. I need peace. I haven't slept in so long. Please help me sleep."

That was the most honest prayer I had ever prayed. And that's all God needed.

He didn't come in fire. He didn't thunder from the heavens. He came as peace. As love. The next thing I remember was being gently lifted to my feet, walking to my bed, lying down, and waking up to first light of the morning warming my face.

It was the best sleep I'd had in years.

That morning, I knew God was real not because of a sermon or a scripture but because He showed up in my room. He shut the voices down. He rescued me.

It marked me. I was different. I didn't know much, but I knew I wanted more of that God, the God who came for me when I had nothing left.

I had blamed the church for everything: the unspoken judgment, the control, the silence, the looks. I blamed God too for what I thought He had taken from me. For letting me hurt. For not stopping her from leaving. For not stopping me from breaking others' hearts..

I had been swinging at everything holy, fighting an unwinnable fight. And the wildest part? God didn't swing back.

He let me get tired.

Tired of hitting His church.

Tired of resenting His people.

Tired of doing the devil's dirty work without even knowing it.

God didn't retaliate. He just watched, waited, and protected. He let the enemy show his hand and watched me come to the end of myself.

I had Him at the moment I whispered, "Hello."

I didn't just encounter a higher power. I met a powerful, loving Father, not a distant one, not a weak one.

A Father who loved fiercely.

A Father who had my back.

A Father who wasn't afraid to invade the darkness I was drowning in.

This wasn't the churchy God I heard about from the pulpit. I met the God who comes into hospital rooms and dark bedrooms. The God who trades suicidal thoughts for supernatural peace. The God who proves His love is not just poetic but powerful. That was the night I stopped fighting God, and started fighting for Him. I fought for our relationship. It was evident in the way I started seeking

Him. I read my Bible on the school bus. I ditched youth group for adult Bible studies. I found an older missionary woman in a retirement home and asked her to disciple me. I threw away music that dragged me back into darkness. I distanced myself from friends who weren't serious about God. I told people what Jesus had done for me.

But then came a new lesson. One that didn't feel as thrilling as the spiritual high from my newfound freedom. It was the art of forgiveness.

Two year had passed since my real conversion experience. I was away in another state at the time, staying with a ministry friend of the family. Things slowed down. Not externally, but internally. God, in His kindness, pumped the brakes on my zealous sprint. Not to stop me but to heal me.

He started tending to my heart, pulling back layers, showing me places I'd ignored. Places still infected with bitterness.

I needed to forgive and not just the obvious enemies but the quiet injuries.

I needed to forgive my father.

I needed to forgive people who made me feel abandoned, rejected, and worthless.

25

I needed to forgive myself—for the dumb decisions, the selfish choices, the pain I caused others while I was in pain myself.

This was new territory for me. I didn't feel ready. I didn't feel like forgiving. But I was willing to be obedient.

God showed me that unforgiveness wasn't just a feeling—it was a wall. A wedge. A spiritual block that kept me from going deeper with Him. That truth hit me hard enough to move me.

I remember reading Robert McGee's book *The Search for Significance* around that time, along with articles about God not just being a King and a Lord, but a Father. A real one. A healing one. One who wanted His children to be whole not just holy.

That revelation laid the groundwork for my true identity to take root. Forgiveness wasn't just about releasing others; it was about restoring me. God was reaching into the messiest corners of my soul. He wasn't afraid to get His hands dirty. He was pulling me out of the orphan spirit and into the spirit of sonship. He wasn't just saving me. He was adopting me. A major test came soon after these lessons when my ex reached out again. She saw the change in me.

We talked. She was curious if we might still have a future together.

But something had shifted.

I cared about her, but I didn't need her. I gave her advice like a friend, not a future. I didn't hint or hope for a reunion. I just wanted her to grow in God. I was still healing and so was she.

That conversation brought closure, a chapter closed with peace.

She eventually married someone else. And surprisingly, it was all good with my soul.

God had something better for me that is a story for another book.

Round 4 | Rope A Dope

A reputation is hard to rebuild.

I had faked people out for so long they didn't know if this new version of me was another act or just a passing phase. I still had chips (plural) on my shoulder. I was driven to prove myself. I had zeal for God, but I don't think many in the church could get past who I had been. Truth is, this new me was new to me too. I was used to being the pastor's kid who was fighting the church, so I kept squaring up.

I started to facilitate a young adult group at my house without going through the proper channels—just passion, a living room, and a drive to lead. But when leadership found out what I was doing—without following the proper protocol—and saw that people were actually showing up, they confronted me.

Now, as a pastor, I understand why that mattered. But back then? I submitted, just not without some resistance.

I also disregarded the process and restarted a group of ministry artists. It was like a Christian Wu-Tang Clan in my head. I wanted to gather talented believers who would disciple one another, sharpen their gifts, and walk through doors God would open to perform. I had vision, drive, and that chip on my shoulder.

It was 1996. I was young, married with two kids, living in an apartment near the church. Getting married wasn't exactly a moment of celebration in my family—at least not at first. We were young. Too young in their eyes. And to be honest, I can't blame them. I was marrying the same young lady I used to crack jokes about in youth group—the one who, at one point, wanted to lay hands on me in a way that wasn't exactly spiritual after I made fun of her friend. But a couple of years, a whole lot of growth, and Jesus in the mix, changed everything. Somewhere between the laughter, the awkward youth group moments, and a shared hunger for God, we grew close.

Still, love didn't exempt us from reality. I had to step up and provide for this new family I was building. So I picked up jobs—working late shifts at

Taco Bell and clocking in hours as a security guard. I was young, clueless, and in over my head—but I was determined. Kids came into the picture almost immediately, which meant that boyhood had to die quick.

Thankfully, the church was just down the street from where we lived, and that gave us something we didn't even know we needed: a community that could help carry the load. Life started moving fast. Faster than I expected. And while I was hoping for overnight progress, God was working through every slow, steady, and sometimes silent season.

I wanted to do things for God—creative, out-of-the-box, inspiring things. But pastoring? Nah. I wasn't trying to be like my dad. Ministry though? That had my heart.

Eventually, I got my first real ministry gig, one with health benefits and a paycheck. I was working with a Mennonite organization doing after-school programs for inner-city youth. The crazy thing is, that ministry had played a part in my dad's spiritual development when he was a kid. It felt like I had come full circle. But I soon realized I didn't know how to manage my time, and I was in over my head—but not alone.

I reached out to a seasoned youth leader who graciously coached me. He gave me a strategy for organizing my time to ensure full, productive days of ministry. That mentorship brought satisfaction and growth. About two years in, I sensed God leading me to transition. They needed someone more experienced, and I needed to see what was next.

My heart was in Philly but after several interviews at different ministries in the area, nothing panned out. Then I got a call about a job in Lancaster, Pennsylvania.

At first, I was skeptical. Out of curiosity, I decided to check it out, and I'm glad I did. That interview turned into a job at Teen Haven. Ironically, this was the ministry that helped lead my dad to Jesus. Another full-circle moment. Working at Teen Haven became one of the greatest spiritual and personal leadership developments I ever experienced.

I was twenty-two. I moved my wife and three kids to Lancaster. We didn't know anyone, and even better, no one knew us. They were meeting the saved version of me. We plugged into a church that was in full-blown revival. It changed everything. People contended for God's presence. The pastor preached fire—messages that broke chains. We were discipled.

We were healed. That church did something wild to my soul.

I went from feeling indifferent about church—or just showing up out of obligation—to becoming fascinated by what it could be and how it could impact my life.

I saw what the church could be—strong, anointed, loving, and powerful. My entire concept of church was being revived. The place I had once resented was becoming the place I wanted to be.

My original plan was to stay a couple years, get some experience, and head back to Philly. But after five years in Lancaster, we were good. We had five kids now, found an affordable home, were plugged into a thriving homeschool community, and had a faith family that loved us well. We didn't want to leave.

Seven years into this good life, I was praying one day, just expressing gratitude to God. I told Him how much I loved young adult ministry and that I'd love to do it for the rest of my life. I sensed the Holy Spirit say, "Tell Me what you love about it."

So I started listing things off, almost like I was reading a job description.

Then He hit me with it.

Everything I said I loved could be summed up in one word: *pastor.*

I was taken aback. For my whole life I had fought the idea of being a pastor. The last thing I wanted was to be like my dad. But God had been doing something behind the scenes. He was preparing me, developing me, and redeeming my broken image of what pastoring looked like.

In that church in Lancaster, God gave me a heart for family restoration. For generational blessings. For city transformation. And I saw that even in its imperfections, the capital *C* Church was still God's answer to a broken world.

Not government programs.

Not politicians.

Not nonprofits.

Not even business ventures.

God's answer has always been… the Church.

And if He wanted me to serve as a pastor, to lead one, then, yes. I was willing.

That yes led me to answer an altar call for those who'd go if God called them. That altar call led to a prophetic word—an urgent call and clarity as to where that call was leading me to go. That word led to a conversation with my pastor. That conversation led to a commissioning to plant a church in Philadelphia.

At thirty years old, I was ordained and sent out to start a church in my hometown.

God won again.

He won my heart—without throwing hands. (Though He did use the laying on of hands to push me in the right direction.)

Round 5 | Rumble in the Jungle

S tarting a church—the very thing I fought against for the first seventeen years of my life—was wild. Bizarre even. Not just for me, but for anyone back in Philly who still remembered who I used to be. And back then, church planting wasn't really a thing in our region. Not like it was in the South or the West where the Bible Belt made it easier. In the Northeast, unless you were backed by a well-established denomination with deep pockets, it was risky business.

Most church planters liked the idea of going to unchurched areas. But Philly? Philly had churches on every corner. Still, not the kind of church I saw in my spirit. Not the kind of church I felt called to build. And I'm sure other planters felt the same about their vision, but this one burned in me.

So I stepped into the ring to start a church in a spiritually challenging part of the city. In a neighborhood where my reputation was shaky at best. In a rough, run-down area. With no steady job. No team. Just some faithful folks as beautifully unaware as I was. We had a storefront building that was falling apart. And a fire in my bones. The fight was on.

A few months before the move, I came down to do some Nehemiah-style recon. Since I was praying about planting in North Philly, I reached out to the former principal of the Christian elementary school I used to attend—yep, the same one who used to paddle me for acting a fool.

There I was, a grown man, married father of five, and a pastor, sitting across from my former elementary school principal at Applebee's. I came to honor him, to show him what God had done in my life, and to tell him I was coming back to the neighborhood—not as a prodigal, but as a pastor. I expected maybe some tears, a "Well done," or a laugh about how all those whuppings weren't in vain.

Instead, he sat me down and hit me with horror stories—raw, unfiltered, and cautionary. Stories of start-up churches that had no guardrails, where passion outran wisdom, and resources were handled recklessly. He spoke of leaders who exploited generosity, mismanaged funds, and burned through people like they were disposable. Then his voice dropped lower as he shared even darker tales—about kids who weren't just overlooked but inappropriately handled, their innocence compromised by the very places meant to protect them.

It wasn't just advice—it was a warning. One soaked in pain, urging me to count the cost of ministry before diving in.

I nodded respectfully, but inside I was fighting discouragement. I thanked him and asked him to pray for us. But that was one of many unwelcoming welcomes I got when I announced I was moving back.

People asked, "Are you serious? Why would you come back here?"

When I started the church, they tried to box me in:

"Are you gonna be an extension of one of the churches you used to go to?"

"Is this a Hispanic church?"

"Are you Baptist? Faith movement? What lane are you in?"

I don't do boxes. Never have.

The fight to start the church wasn't just about logistics. It was about restoring my reputation. Proving that I was a man after God's heart for this city. Showing people that I wanted to serve—not compete with—the people of God already here. But I wasn't trying to do what was already being done. God gave me something from the future, something irreligious, something creative.

I had some experience and a lot of passion but no blueprint. I don't think anyone is ever fully prepared for where God sends them. But I was learning to stay full of faith for what I couldn't yet see.

Eventually, I found work. We moved our fledgling church into that busted old storefront, and to our surprise, people started showing up—families looking for hope, backsliders ready to try again, and friends curious about what we were building in that busted storefront. Later on others came: people hungry for more of God. I prayed hard. Cried hard. Fought hard. I wasn't just trying to build a church. I was contending for a city.

I started showing up at pastors' meetings and denominational gatherings, looking for what God was already doing that I could come alongside, but the groups were tribal. I don't mean that in a negative way. There wasn't much crossover. The Hispanic tribe gathered. The denominational tribes gathered. But where was the mosaic? Where were the spaces where all tribes could sit at the same table?

That hunger birthed the Shepherds Club—a space for diverse pastors and leaders to come together with one agenda: the kingdom. Not church growth, not denominational pride, not because of style or structure, just a deep desire to see God's kingdom advance. It became a space where leaders could connect, feel safe, and know they're not alone. The motto was: we're better together.

I was in my early thirties but looked like a kid. Even in a suit, people were confused.

"That's the pastor?" they'd ask.

At weddings, people thought I was the DJ.

Our church was unorthodox to say the least. We had a disco ball we'd turn on during worship. People didn't know what to do with that. And honestly, that was the point. I was fighting to make sure religion didn't feel comfortable in our house.

The early years were a blur of activity:

- Street outreaches

- Prayer walks
- Talk-show-style talent nights
- Healing services
- Out-of-the-box worship
- Original dramas
- Services in after-hours venues
- Teaching people how to hear God prophetically
- Twenty-four-hour prayer and fasting concerts

We moved seven times in seven years as we outgrew buildings and found new opportunities. Eventually, I hired staff with no outside funding. We were 100 percent supported by the people. And these were mostly blue-collar—or no-collar—folks, young, inner-city families, and they were generous.

We got to a point where signs, wonders, and miracles were normal.

The hunger was real.

The humility in leadership was rare.

And the honor in the house was rich.

Other ministries admired us.

Some were suspicious.

Some just didn't know what to do with us.

But I was just fighting for the church to be a city on a hill.

Fighting for unity among leaders.

Fighting for revival.

The kiss of redemption during that time came in the form of all the types of people I had wounded in the past. Jesus was now using me to help bring healing. Instead of people walking into our church and experiencing a wounded pastor's kid who added salt to their wounds, they were encountering a healed pastor who wanted nothing more than for them to experience the healing, restorative power of our heavenly Father.

It was wild! Addicted ex-cons were finding freedom. Violent individuals were being rocked by the peace of God. People bound by witchcraft were being delivered. A powerful moment came when there was someone struggling with depression and suicidal thoughts. I could feel it in the room. A woman, overwhelmed with emotion, came forward to be set free. The power of God changed her life. It was during this time when I first discerned and called out the very spirit that had been abusing me for years. Now

God was using me to fight off the very spirit that once almost knocked me out.

People from my past—those I went to youth group with, those who had backslid—now called me pastor. Family members I had hurt gave me another chance. This was the redemption I never saw coming.

Yes, I made mistakes. I allowed some things during those revival years that would later come back to bite us. I wasn't fully prepared for the level of warfare that comes when you're taking enemy ground. The devil wasn't sending feather-weight demons anymore. We were battling the heavyweights.

The attacks were strategic. The enemy targeted the head. Then the body. And as the head dropped its guard to protect the body, the enemy landed a hook that sent the whole thing reeling.

Around year thirteen, I found myself in the fight of my life.

What came next was a fight I never saw coming— this time, with the very ones we had contended for and helped restore in Christ. They were still just kids in the Kingdom, learning to walk, but now they were swinging.

PASTOR vs CHURCH KIDS

Round 1 | Shadow Boxing

From 2018-2023, life was drained from me. Some individuals who once confessed love and allegiance turned away. They put on an appearance of humility and even enticed others to follow their departure. It was devastating. I still loved them, but I felt deep disappointment as everything I thought was stable crumbled around me.

Was I truly experiencing what my accusers claimed: that God's hand was no longer on my life? I prayed. I pleaded with the Lord to examine me through His Word and through the wisdom of trusted people in my life. I asked Him to reveal what I was blind to. My confidence was shattered. My passion for ministry dwindled.

I felt the need to protect my wife from the darker parts of my struggles. Many who were no longer connected to me remained connected to her, and I didn't want to force her into a position of choosing sides. I knew she loved both me and them, but it only deepened my sense of isolation. It made me feel like I was the problem.

I had to bite my tongue while false narratives about me circulated, spread by people I once considered family. I watched as those with even a hint of empathy for me were placed in difficult and precarious situations. I longed to be understood, but how could I? To explain my side would have felt like self-defense, and it would have placed me in opposition to others. I knew this battle wasn't against flesh and blood.

So much was stripped away. Waves of anxiety robbed me of sleep, while depression left me wanting only to escape into a cave. The verbal jabs and online attacks didn't hit all at once. They came in waves. Rumors and secondhand whispers trickled in from people I trusted, casting doubt on my ability to lead well or spiritually feed those who were genuinely hungry for God's word. It wasn't a sudden storm but a slow, creeping tide of suspicion that tried to undermine what God was building through the church. Then it came in relentless waves. Just when I felt relief, another blow would strike.

I needed people more than ever, yet my trust in others was at an all-time low. It seemed every meeting on my calendar was just another goodbye. People came to tell me they were leaving, and the enemy used this to convince me that I was no longer anyone's pastor—just a glorified doorman, ushering people to their next church. The depth of fellowship I once enjoyed was gone. The respect, the honor—it was all a shadow of what it used to be.

The revival that once burned brightly was now reduced to ashes. I knew the dangers of anchoring my identity in anything outside of Christ, but that truth didn't quiet the war raging within me. I held fast to the knowledge that God is good, gracious, and abounding in love. Yet, even as I worked to populate heaven, I felt as though I was simultaneously populating other churches with people who used to be part of ours.

We couldn't afford to do the things we used to because so many of our dependable givers had moved on. Another leader would step down, or someone would bring an urgent emergency to my attention. My family faced its own crises. I began to wonder conflicting thoughts: Am I cursed or blessed? Why do the unrighteous seem to prosper? And am I so arrogant to think that I am the only righteous one?

The leaders who remained were dealing with their own struggles and didn't have the capacity to pull me out of my present darkness. I cried out, "God, why me?" I felt the weight of condemnation for all the ways I didn't measure up, for all the people I had failed. Was it possible that my antagonists were right? Had I been deceived all along?

My children were grown and out of the house, yet I didn't want to remain in a home that had hosted so many who now felt like strangers. I tried to convince myself it wasn't trauma, but it was. I was traumatized.

At first, I thought it would last only a few months, maybe a year. Surely the Lord would bring me out. But another year passed, and then another. Each time hope began to rise, it was stripped away by yet another crisis. Like clockwork, just after hearing that one of our most trusted and dependable families was relocating out of state, I got word from the landlord that we had to vacate the building we had poured over eight years of sweat, prayer, manpower, and finances into. My response? A dry, sarcastic "Of course" because by then, it felt like loss had become routine. Eventually, I became numb to the bad news.

It felt like my fault. I was convinced that I did what I had an inner determination never to do. I killed a church in revival. I sacrificed my family on the altar of ministry. I prioritized programs over people. Like Job, it felt as if I had unknowingly committed some mysterious offense—something so serious it seemed unforgivable.

This was my reality: walking, breathing, and barely leading, and fighting the shadows in my inner world.

Round 2 | Against the Ropes

How did it come to this? How did I end up estranged from people I once considered family? I'm not here to blame or point fingers. I want to take a hard, honest look at how I got here.

Rewind to when I started the church. I was young—just thirty years old—when I began pastoring. I believed my experiences prepared me to return to the badlands of Philadelphia to start a church God had called me to plant. Yet, I was still a rookie trying to do something new and unprecedented. Most Christians I knew couldn't help me because I was stepping into a vision that was uncharted territory. On top of that, I returned to a city where I was already carrying baggage—a pain-in-the-neck pastor's kid with a bad reputation.

I remember it like it was yesterday. There was no financial reservoir, no local support. It was just raw faith being tested at every turn. As the church grew, I took on the responsibility of building a team—onboarding staff and pastors to help carry the vision. But now, with resources steadily diminishing, I felt the heavy burden of trying to financially sustain the very people who had committed their lives to serve alongside me. What once felt like momentum now felt like weight, pressing hard on my shoulders. I cried often in those early days. It didn't take long to realize I didn't have the skills to handle all that was required of me. I was in over my head, under constant pressure, and trying to carry it all with grace.

After a couple of years searching for relief, I had brutal conversations with a few people I cared about. Along the journey, I learned a hard lesson about second-hand trauma. I didn't even know what that was at first. But it's real—and it happens when someone is affected not by what they went through, but by what you share with them. I'm an outward processor, especially with people I consider safe. I don't come to them with everything figured out. I talk to work things out. Often, I'd share my inner wrestlings about people's intentions or behaviors, trying to make sense of patterns or decisions. It wasn't gossip; it was evaluation. But what I didn't realize was that the weight of my processing was too much for some people. They weren't built to carry it, and it shook their confidence in me. It made them quietly wonder, *If something goes wrong between us, will our relationship fall apart too?* I was seeking clarity, but unintentionally I created confusion. And now I know—not everyone can or should be that kind of sounding board. That was a big regret.

Fast-forward a bit, and my leadership style—marked by candor and authenticity—became a double-edged sword. In the beginning, people appreciated my raw honesty, but when they felt it was directed at them, the appreciation turned to offense. They loved the bold, audacious steps I took to build something new, but when it disrupted their comfort, they felt used.

Bad habits began to emerge, masked by my zeal for ministry. I created programs to serve people and help them serve others, but I neglected to ensure the leaders were truly caring for their teams. I assumed they were, but they weren't. People began to feel used—not by the church as a whole, but by individuals within it. Instead of addressing these issues one-on-one, they threw indirect shade at the church as a whole. It's easier to attack an institution than to confront a person.

We were pioneering something new, learning on the fly, and failing to prepare people for the inevitable backlash. What started as strengths in one season became weaknesses in the next because we didn't season our zeal with wisdom and grace.

Ironically, I was sent to heal the religiously wounded, yet we became a place where people were being wounded. I gathered elders and a board to help me, but they were as inexperienced as I was. They looked to me for guidance, but I didn't slow down enough to seek a spiritual father or mentor to guide me in return. Early ignorance turned into bad habits.

People tried to split the church in those formative years, and I didn't always handle it well. To those who experienced that side of my leadership and left limping, I'm sorry. Some who were hurt during that time haven't recovered. I take responsibility for being a young, passionate thirtysomething-year-old who loved Jesus, lived for revival, and brought in the harvest but didn't know how to care for the laborers.

In the beginning, love covered a multitude of sins. But as the love simmered, cracks began to show. Even the prophetic gift I championed—the gift I made room for—turned against me. "Making room for the gift" had been our language—a symbolic but sincere way of creating space in our church services for those with prophetic gifting to be used by God.

Prophetic gifts in our church context were more than just moments of spiritual expression—they were deeply personal and often powerful. These gifts included receiving visions—glimpses of what God was doing or about to do in someone's life or in the church at large. Others had a sensitivity to God's voice that allowed them to speak words of encouragement or direction to individuals, often saying exactly what someone needed to hear in the moment. Some had a knack for interpreting dreams, helping people make sense of the spiritual symbolism they were experiencing in the night. These weren't just emotional impressions; many times, these words, visions, and interpretations carried a weight that confirmed what someone had been praying about or revealed what was going on beneath the surface. When healthy and humble, prophetic gifts created awe, clarity, and connection to God's heart.

We wanted people to grow in their callings, to be activated, to hear from heaven and release it in the room. But somewhere along the way, that room I had made became a platform for something else. The same prophetic voices I had once encouraged and empowered slowly shifted. They began forming tight-knit alliances with others in the church, and when conflict arose, they didn't step in to reconcile or bring clarity. Instead, they became the "safe" space where people could vent, process offense, and find agreement in their grievances. What was meant to be a source of spiritual edification became a magnet for division cloaked in discernment. The very gifts I had fought to make space for were now being used—intentionally or not—in ways that worked against me and the unity of the house.

It started subtly, cloaked in spiritual innocence, which made it even more dangerous. I didn't know how to address it and ended up letting suspicion and resentment creep into my life. I didn't have hard evidence—just instinct and discernment—but it was enough to plant seeds of doubt in me. This was the beginning of a slippery slope. The prophetic gifts were legitimate and necessary, but I didn't lead through the challenges they presented well. That failure would haunt me in the years to come.

This is the raw reality of how it began to unravel. I was young, unprepared, and learning as I went. But the weight of those missteps—both mine and others'—paved the road to where I was heading in the next couple of years.

Round 3 | Sloppy Footwork

We experienced so many good years. It was a creative, Spirit-filled, youthful environment that breathed life into everything we did. Maybe that's why on the streets we weren't known as a church but as "Club Jesus"—a place that felt more like a party than a sanctuary. It was the kind of place preachers wanted to come to because the response was electric. Our stage was alive with enthusiasm, and our pews were filled with expectant hearts.

We weren't just a church; we were a movement. Other churches came to see what God was doing. Pastors sought out our leaders to recruit them into their own ministries. Politicians called us when they wanted to reach the largest demographic of Hispanic families in the city. Here's the kicker: we didn't even have a substantial sign on our building. We relied on word of mouth, not slick marketing.

There were moments that still make me smile—like the times we had lines of people outside waiting to get in for special events, the concerts, the speakers such as the legendary Nicky Cruz. Testimonies poured in of lives being changed: healings, deliverances, salvations. We welcomed young families, embraced diversity, and even saw large financial gifts that made our work possible. It felt like heaven was touching earth.

Back then, I wasn't depleted or defeated. I was alive with vision. I was optimistic about the future, surrounded by a team of energetic people who shared my fire. Together, we were ready to storm the next mountain.

But there was an hourglass of sand I couldn't see—each grain quietly sliding down. I wouldn't realize until later that this was the beginning of a countdown to a couple major fallouts.

Halloween was always a time when the devil seemed to take center stage. We decided to flip the script. If the devil was going to get attention, we'd use it to expose him.

We created a live production that pulled no punches. It told raw, unfiltered stories of people making seemingly innocent decisions while demons pulled the strings in the background. The play exposed how natural actions carried devastating spiritual, eternal consequences. Scenes of sexual compromise, drug addiction, and brokenness hit close to home. The spiritual realm was unveiled in a way that gripped the audience.

It was powerful. People were delivered from unclean spirits, saved, and set free. It seemed like a huge victory.

Then, just weeks later, everything began to unravel. One by one, the people involved in the production started to fall off. It was as if they were becoming the characters they portrayed on stage. Scandals erupted; adultery, betrayals, secret sins all came to light. Families were under attack. It was chaos.

My instinct was to address it head-on, not to sweep it under the rug. I wanted restoration for everyone involved, protection for the vulnerable, and healing for the wounded. But not everyone wanted to be restored. Some took their process into their own hands.

We were all traumatized by what had happened. Looking back, it felt like the story of Tamar and Absalom in the Bible. King David's daughter Tamar was violated by her half-brother Amnon. When

King David didn't handle it the way his son Absalom thought he should, Absalom took matters into his own hands. He killed Amnon and later turned his anger toward David, plotting to overthrow his kingdom. It felt like the story of Tamar all over again—but this time, Tamar was the Church.

She was supposed to be cherished, protected, and honored. Instead, she was violated. The abuse didn't always look like what we read in 2 Samuel 13, but the spirit of it was the same. Amnon—like some in positions of church authority—used his access to harm instead of to heal. He represented those who abused power under the guise of ministry, leaving behind spiritual confusion and deep emotional wounds.

Then there was Absalom—the one who took up Tamar's pain as his own. I saw this spirit in people who, driven by righteous anger, turned to rebellion rather than reconciliation. They couldn't just stand by and watch injustice unfold, so they took matters into their own hands, often tearing down the very thing they once loved in the process.

And David? He was the leader. The one with authority and spiritual responsibility, but for some reason, he stayed silent. Whether it was fear, passivity, or simply not knowing what to do, his inaction spoke volumes. And too many modern leaders, myself included at times, have mirrored David's mistake—overlooking glaring issues in the name of peace, unity, or self-preservation.

But just like in the biblical narrative, the silence and mishandling only led to deeper division. And when the church becomes Tamar, it should break our hearts enough to do something about it—not cover it up, not explain it away, and definitely not weaponize the pain for personal gain. A spirit of Absalom was destroying the family.

Absalom is like family—the last person you'd suspect. He has access to the inner circle, and he's charismatic, talented, and persuasive. But his mission is to manipulate covenants and allegiances toward himself.

It started with chatter. Leaders I had entrusted with influence began to shift. They loved being part of the church and our home, but suddenly, some didn't like the pace at which the ministry was moving. Others quietly disagreed with our moral stance on issues that had become heavily politicized. What began as minor grievances—like the absence of ministries tailored to their specific needs—slowly grew into major points of contention. Small preferences became dividing lines. And what once felt like unity began to unravel in subtle but significant ways.

Their language changed, and their discontent spread like wildfire.

The spirit of Absalom didn't stop with one person. It moved through senior leaders, deacons, intercessors, the worship team, youth group, and young adults. It created an exodus—leaders influencing others to leave with them. I watched people go, one after another, including some I thought would never leave.

Some groups never returned. Not one person from those groups became a bridge builder or brought life back to the family. It was as if they'd vanished into another world.

Like David, all I could do retreat back to my corner. I was dethroned in the hearts of the people. I was dazed by church family trauma.

Looking back, I see my mistakes. I elevated people too quickly. I placed them in positions of influence before their character had been tested. The Bible warns us not to lay hands on people too quickly (1 Timothy 5:22), but in my pursuit of progress, I neglected process.

I did a lot right, but I did some things wrong despite my best efforts. God gets the blame when things go right. The devil gets blamed when things go wrong. The truth is I have to own the wrong outcomes as the chief steward, or should I say chief scientist? The line between a brilliant pioneer and a mad scientist is thin and easy to cross. People with certain gift sets and personality traits teeter on the line of being Einstein or Frankenstein. Both are brilliant and both have had failures despite their brilliance. It's when things go wrong in the holy experiments and when we start to build the church in our image rather than the image of Christ that things begin to unravel. And now the monster, your creation, sets out to destroy its maker just like in the classic novel.

Principles of church success are popular. Principles of shrinkage are accidentally practiced. I want to purposely share with you the missteps I had along the way to help you avoid them. I believe the sloppy footwork contributed to the years of regression. It can take a while for what a person to reap what he has sown. The consequences of certain actions came later down the road.

10 Body Shots

Lagging male leadership: While having anointed and competent women in ministry is a blessing. The Lord was showing me the weight or burden of the ministry needs to have an adequate number of anointed and competent men to carry it. We had so many women in key positions that when warfare got intense, it took emotional and spiritual toil that needed godly men to bring us through. It is easier to find willing alpha women in our urban settings than it is to find alpha males whose identity in Christ is intact and who lead with confidence and grace. So many times we do the easy thing. God showed me easy now will turn unhealthy later.

Spending money on the wrong things: In my eagerness to see our place beautified, I spent more money on reconstruction than on mission. It wasn't reckless spending; it just wasn't prioritizing our purpose as a ministry. We exist to make disciples of Christ. Part of making disciples is making sure we go out and seek and save the lost. The more we spend on getting staff, the lazier I saw the capable volunteers become.

Elevating people too quickly: Instead of teaching and developing people personally and taking time to ensure their souls were whole and they were spiritually maturity, I put people in charge before they were ready. When you use people where they are at, they think they are further along than they really are. No one betrayed me; I betrayed myself into believing something about them that I hadn't taken the time to really see. It resulted in people building a ministry on the side instead of building up the body they were apart of. Me giving roles to those who showed a level of being faithful but had not yet been fruitful. Ministry assignments were being stewarded by talented orphans. Talented orphans get their identity in their performance and not in who they are in Christ.

Prioritizing outreach over prayer-reach: When we were going out to advance the Kingdom of God through outreach efforts or evangelize the lost, I didn't account for the backlash the enemy would bring due to us invading his territory. Our church had a team of intercessors but what we were going after needed corporate prayer coverage. It's important to prioritize prayer for a ministry to succeed in Kingdom advancment.

Slowing down to appease people: There was a time that we had mid-week service and small group gatherings during the week. There was so much going on that testimonies where hard to keep up with. People were engaged and alive with what God was doing. God impressed upon me to cut back on the events and have more substantial gatherings. We did that for a season. Then when I sensed we had to pick up the pace again, certain leaders pushed against it. As a result of slowing down on mid-week meetings, it created a void for people who were desiring connection, development, and ministry, so they went elsewhere.

Being ungracious to those who take advantage: This might sound weird to say but I have a hard time giving grace to those who are deceptive and causing disorder. I would become very combative if people would have an approach to their decisions that wasn't bibically congurent. This caused many people that just wanted to move on to feel manipulated or attacked or not trusted. I assumed they were coming to me for guidance. They weren't. They were coming to me to bless what they already decided they wanted to do. I have learned sometimes it's more gracious to say goodbye than give someone the spiritual riot act.

Losing my confidence: When I couldn't be what people wanted me to be, it caused me to fall into a depression. I was in the predicament of having a level of responsibility I had never had before without having the support I need to share the pressure with me. My gifts had gone into hiding because my confidence and sense of competence flatlined. My soul needed a Savior. My identity as a son had to be rebuilt.

Lacking discipleship for new believers: Our system to connect people into discipleship wasn't thought through very well. So many people were coming in the doors and getting saved, but they would flounder. They served but weren't being discipled. They attended services but weren't being shepherded. It showed especially when the storms of life hit; they would drown in the waters of despair rather than take authority over the storm. We should have personally guided them better in what Christ has giving them and what they can do to overcome what was overwhelming them.

Poorly modeling rest and recuperating: After experiencing waves of loss or challenges, we need time to recuperate. The relentless cycle of ministry comes with hellos and goodbyes and crises. It's important to take time to restore the wounded, beaten, and battered. For our mental and spiritual health, we need to be replenished and be ministered to by Jesus frequently. A rhythm of rest makes sure condemnation or shame don't take over. Jesus teaches us how to lead through conflict with grace while gently restoring identity and purpose in our lives. By not giving people the time to let their souls be whole or their spiritual maturity catch up with their roles, this created a fertile ground for the spirit of Absalom to take root.

Neglecting the family altar: Safeguarding family relationships in the midst of ministry demands is no easy task. Balancing ministry activities with healthy boundaries shows your family they are loved and cherished.

For the years that followed the fallouts, I wandered. I preached, but I could tell the people weren't with me. I led, but their hearts weren't all-in. They were going through the motions, and so was I for the most part.

I wrestled with whether to step away. While other pastors in other churches were leaving the ministry for reasons like infidelity or financial misconduct. That wasn't me. I had stayed pure before the Lord. I had been transparent with our finances. I wasn't burned out, yet I was bleeding while leading.

I kept telling myself to give it one more year. Don't make an emotional decision in the middle of the storm. Surely this season would pass. But I didn't anticipate how long it would take—or how deeply wounded I was.

Round 4 | Comeback Kid

There I was, years removed from the high points and hard hits, standing in the rubble of what had been and the framework of what was becoming. I was stripped of so much—positions, people, illusions—but entrusted with even more. Two coffeehouses were in my care. I had become a landlord. The baton of a national church fellowship had been passed to me. We had finally acquired our first permanent building for the church. I was stewarding citywide unity efforts, covering spiritual sons and daughters, and supporting leaders drawn to our church network. All while trying to get my footing again.

This was the tension I lived in: rebuilding without repeating. I was pacing myself to see the latter house become greater than the former. And yet, even as blessings surrounded me, the residue of battle fatigue still clung to my soul. After a long, drawn-out building fundraiser that took far more out of me than I ever imagined, my faith felt worn thin. I had been running through quicksand for years. Now I was finally still enough to breathe—and breathe I did. Deep, exhausted, grateful breaths.

It was in that stillness, in between gasps for spiritual air, that I realized if it weren't for God's mercy, I wouldn't have made it. The luster of leadership had faded. The spotlight didn't thrill me anymore. I didn't want another platform. I just wanted Jesus. I wanted to be with Him. To see His eyes looking at me. Not the me with the titles or vision boards, but the beat-up, limping, tear-streaked version of me.

I couldn't help but think of Peter. After his betrayal, he went back to what he knew: fishing. But when he saw Jesus on the shore, he didn't wait for the boat to dock. He dove in and swam, exhausted, desperate, undone. I was Peter, swimming with tired arms just to fall at the feet of the only One who made the world worth enduring. And like with Peter, Jesus didn't scold me. He cooked me breakfast. He fed my weary soul with exactly what it needed.

In His gaze, I started seeing again. Not just looking—seeing. I saw the beauty of brokenness. I saw the eternal weight of glory behind my temporary afflictions. I saw how my confidence was never meant to be in the work of my hands but in the One whose hands bore the nails. The fight wasn't over, but somehow I already felt like I'd won . . . because of who was in my corner.

Then came the tests.

One sweet couple we had walked closely with met with us to let us know—gently—that their time with us had come to a close. My response? Peace. Gratitude. Release. Not panic. Not spiraling. Just peace. Another family we'd weathered ups and downs with over the years eventually said their goodbyes too. Again, my spirit didn't sink. I was steady. Thankful. Confident in Christ, not dependent on people.

I started noticing the people who stayed , their faithfulness, their sacrifice. They had Jesus in their eyes. Then, almost like a divine wink, people who had left years ago began to return. Instead of suspicion, I felt joy. Why? Because I'd finally grasped a simple, freeing truth: This isn't my church. I'm not the builder. Jesus is. He said He would build His church. My job is to let Him do His job. That means some things are scaffolding; some things are structure. My freedom came in surrendering the blueprint back to the Architect.

My soul started coming back to life. A two-month sabbatical with my wife helped shift everything. In that extended abiding, I realized God was giving me endurance—not just for the blessings, but for the burdens that came with them. He was increasing my capacity. And because so much of my flesh had already been crucified in previous seasons, the new sacrifices didn't sting the same. I wasn't flinching anymore. I trusted God—even with my "Isaac."

This, I believe, is what seasoned surrender looks like. There's a wisdom God gives only on the other side of obedience. And I was hungry for it. My fight now is not for status, not for outcomes, but for purity of fellowship with my Father. My fight is to guard the peace that comes from righteous living. To build systems that reflect grace, growth, and accountability. To maintain faith in the One who already won the war.

If you're a pastor or leader reading this and are feeling burnt out, beaten down, ready to quit, I want to tell you: There's a comeback in you. The fight is real. And it's spiritual. That's why Paul told Timothy:

> "Fight the good fight of faith. Take hold of the eternal life to which you were called and have confessed the good confession in the presence of many witnesses." (1 Timothy 6:12)

"God has not given us a spirit of fear, but of power, and of love, and of a sound mind." (2 Timothy 1:7)

"Endure hardship as a good soldier of Jesus Christ." (2 Timothy 2:3)

We're in a battle that requires armor and weapons, and we've been given both. And a Captain who knows how to lead us to victory. Find your corner. Know who's coaching you. Get around other warriors because when you're surrounded by people on cruise control while you're still in the trenches, it can wear you down.

Take heart. God prepares a table for you in the presence of your enemies (Psalm 23:5). While warfare rages, God is feeding and refreshing you in full view of hell. That's what it means to be a son, a soldier, and a servant all at once. Sometimes the very church you're called to lead feels like it's crucifying you. And like Jesus, we lay our lives down for her anyway.

We grow weary because we fight *against* the church rather than *for* her. Or worse, we develop an unhealthy soul-tie to the ministry and forget who it belongs to. But when I surrendered it all—again—I found supernatural wisdom and strength.

Our souls get tired, but they also get revived. If we fight for them to abide with the Lover of our souls, we will find rest and redemption. The comeback starts there—not in fixing everything, but in returning to Him.

I'm the comeback kid because I came back to His feet. I came back to His lap. And my good Father lavished His love on me. That's where I found my fight again.

That's where I found who He created me to be again.

COMEBACK KID vs CHURCH CULTURE

Round 1 | The Golden Gloves

One Sunday, after a powerful service, I invited those in need of healing to come forward. The response was overwhelming—a long line of people seeking a touch from God. As I prayed, faith filled the room. Someone with one leg shorter than the other was sitting on the platform. This wasn't just a minor ailment; this was a moment where God's power would either be evident or absent. Just as we prepared to pray, the entire building lost power.

Silence fell. The glow of emergency exit lights barely lit the room. I felt the weight of uncertainty, but before I could react, phone flashlights began flickering on, illuminating the stage. Then a murmur turned into a roar as people began to pray with fervor. Faith was rising in the dark.

I gave people permission to leave, but no one moved. We were going to be the light in the darkness.

As the flashlights shone on the woman's legs, I declared God's healing. Before I could lay hands on her, we all saw it—the shorter leg extended, evening out before our very eyes. Gasps, shouts, and applause filled the air. That night, miracle after miracle unfolded, not because of a well-planned program, but because we contended for the presence of God.

The Gold Standard: Presence over Everything

God is the gold standard. His presence is our first and highest priority, the non-negotiable core of who we are and what we do. Everything else—people, programs, and property—follows after Him in order of importance. When we get this hierarchy right, everything functions as it should. When we get it wrong, we risk becoming just another institution, void of the power and presence of God.

The phrase "gold standard" comes from the historical use of gold to back national currencies, representing the highest level of value, purity, and trust. In the world of sports, the gold medal represents the highest achievement. It's the ultimate reward for excellence, sacrifice, and mastery. Athletes train for years with the singular goal of standing on the top podium, receiving gold, because it symbolizes being the very best in the world. Silver and bronze, while still honors, are lesser honors because gold is more rare, resilient, and radiant—making it the perfect symbol of victory. Silver and bronze, though valuable, simply don't carry the same weight of prestige or perfection.

The Bible gives us a striking example of what happens when we mishandle God's presence. In 2 Samuel 6, King David wanted to bring the ark of the covenant—the very representation of God's presence—back to Jerusalem. His heart was in the right place, but his method was all wrong. Instead of following God's instructions for how to carry the ark—carried by Levites using special poles that were through rings on the ark—David put the ark on a cart pulled by oxen. It was efficient, it was practical, and it was a disaster waiting to happen.

As the procession moved forward, the oxen stumbled, and Uzzah, trying to steady the ark, reached out and touched it. He was struck dead instantly. The celebration turned into a funeral. Why? Because David had put the program before the presence. He wanted to expedite the process, to make it easier, but in doing so, he neglected the reverence required for God's presence.

This is a sobering reminder for every church leader who gets their own version of an ox cart—placing convenience over consecration. We build impressive programs, well-oiled systems, and seamless productions, but if they are not carried by the right people, with the right reverence, we risk spiritual disaster. Programs should never carry the weight of what only God's presence was meant to sustain.

When David saw what had happened, he abandoned the mission, afraid of what more could go wrong. The ark was left in the house of a man named Obed-Edom, and something incredible happened: his entire household was blessed. Why? Because when the presence of God is properly housed and honored, blessings follow. When David realized this, he corrected his approach. The next time, he did it God's way. The Levites carried the ark, and David worshiped with abandon. The result? The presence of God was brought into Jerusalem with joy, power, and blessing.

The Danger of Secondary Priorities

Prioritizing God's presence isn't just theological smart; it's a safeguard against letting secondary things take first place. Many churches claim that God is their priority, but their actions tell a different story.

People should get the silver. Relationships, community, and discipleship are essential, but they must never replace God as our source. Some churches are people-driven, catering to the preferences and comfort of the crowd. They build impressive teams, organize massive outreach efforts, and fund incredible missions. But people, even in the name of Jesus, can build without God. A people-first church risks silencing hard truths and avoiding anything that challenges their audience. They may do good things but miss the God things.

Programs get the bronze. Having well-run systems, ministries, and outreach initiatives is important, but they are a means to an end, not the end itself. Some churches are program-driven—structured down to the minute. Five minutes of announcements, eight minutes of praise, four minutes of worship, a TED Talk-style sermon, and a scripted closing prayer. Everything is predictable, comfortable, and polished. But God isn't predictable. When He moves, it often disrupts people's plans. Program-driven churches struggle to make room for divine interruptions.

The truth is, when programs take priority over presence, they may appear successful in the world's eyes, but they lack the spiritual power to bring lasting change. Just like David's first attempt to transport the ark, many churches push forward, building their ox carts, trusting in their own ingenuity rather than divine instruction. And when the weight becomes too great, things collapse.

But when God is first, even the simplest house— like Obed-Edom's—becomes a place of divine blessing. Honoring God means giving Him room, making sure He doesn't have to share His space with anything or anyone else. When we give God the room, we watch Him move in ways no program, personality, or property ever could.

Honorable Mention: Property

Buildings and facilities matter. They house our gatherings, serve our communities, and provide a place for ministry. But when property becomes the priority, churches turn into monuments of past moves of God rather than facilitators of fresh encounters. The pristine sanctuary must remain untouched, and ministry programs are filtered through the lens of what won't disturb the carpet or equipment. These churches become museums rather than movements.

Why Presence Comes First

At our church, we have chosen a different way. Prioritizing God's presence doesn't mean attracting the biggest crowds, but it does mean we create space for real transformation. When we make room for Him, for miracles to happen, lives to change, and cities to awaken to His power.

This isn't about dismissing people, programs, or property—they all have their place. But when God's presence is first, everything else aligns. We don't invite people into a well-run organization; we invite them into an encounter with the living God. And that changes everything.

Round 2 | The Crowd Goes Wild

Let me take you back to one of the most unforgettable moments in live television: Miss Universe 2015. The world is watching. Cameras are flashing. Hearts are racing. Dreams are on the line. Steve Harvey, standing under the bright lights, makes the climactic announcement: "Miss Universe 2015 is … Miss Colombia!" The crowd erupts. Confetti falls. The crown is placed. The sash is draped. But just minutes later—gut punch—Harvey comes back on stage, visibly shaken, and utters the words that would go down in broadcast history: "I have to apologize." He had announced the wrong winner. The crown wasn't meant for Miss Colombia. It was meant for Miss Philippines. That single slip-up became a global spectacle. The wrong person had been crowned. The real winner stood off to the side, overlooked, as the world applauded the one never meant to wear the crown.

That's exactly what I see happening in the Church today.

We've put people—podcasters, celebrity personalities, and even pastors—in the winner's circle. We've crowned charisma while God stands quietly in the wings, waiting to be honored. People were never meant to win the gold. According to heaven's order, people are silver. Valuable, essential, worth serving and celebrating, but never meant to be first. When people become first place, we create a church culture that's off-kilter, and the world is watching us crown the wrong one. It creates confusion, drama, and disillusionment in the Church and outside of it. The One who was always meant to take center stage— God alone—is being treated like the runner-up.

We need a Steve Harvey moment in the Church. A moment where we pause the show, step back in humility, and admit, "We got it wrong." We need to remove the crown from the one who was never meant to wear it and return the highest honor to the One who deserves it: God. That's when we see real transformation. That's when the Church will rediscover its power.

For me to tell you to put people second might sound like I'm antisocial. Nothing could be further from the truth. Nothing invigorates me more than meeting new people. I am so into getting to know new people that while the national shut down was happening and we had to pivot from in-person ministry (which didn't stop us from meeting though lots of people were hesitant to return), we acquired two coffeehouses. The launching of those business was a joy. Customers would come in and tell us their stories. I love people. I love to hear their stories. I love making connections and connecting others to communities that will enhance their life. My wife will attest to meeting people all over the world because I just strike up conversations. I encourage my adult children to build meaningful connections with every person God brings into their lives, recognizing that each relationship could serve a divine purpose. At the church I do everything in my power to not get belligerent with my introvert leaders who don't go out of their way to interact with the newer people.

People coming in second just means that they are not going to be treated better than our heavenly Father when we gather. When we do that right, people should never feel second class. Being second also means they are not our source; they are not who we are led by and so on.

"This place is so welcoming" is one of the common statements we get from first-time guests. It is a testament to how we want people to know they are seen and important.

When we put people second behind God, we then can begin to find ways to invest and connect with them so that they find their place in the house of God. We can work with them to find out how to best meet their needs. Instead of shoving people in programs the pastors and staff created, we could help them put together a program that would best help meet their needs. If we have a ton of widowed seniors, we create programs that they would want to participate in. Tailoring programs to the people is a way of meeting people where they are.

If our programs are higher in priority than our people, we miss the unique skillsets and needs of the people who have chosen to do life with us. The key is to find the right set of leaders who have the capacity, competency, character, and core values you have to serve those people through the programs.

Being in the people business is so multifaceted. Especially when there are different generations represented and then add onto that the different cultural backgrounds. One needs great agility to keep leading people effectively when they can be so unpredictable. People go through whole life cycles in front of your eyes if they are there long enough.

They go from a giddy teenager to serious young adult, to a settled-down married person, and then to a family man or woman. Their interests and availability changes, which are things we are not always prepared for. My point is that you have to put God first to best deal with the unpredictability that comes when people change up on you. It is easier to have the presence of God to help you navigate the ever-changing dynamics of people then putting people so high up that when they are fickle or absent then everything doesn't come crumbling down.

Round 3 | It's Showtime

No one would argue that having small groups is one of the most important community-building and disciple-making programs we can have in our church. But there are so many approaches, styles, and names to the small groups. We call ours Circles. Because circles are better than rows. Having these programs takes people from just hanging out in the crowd to becoming engaged participants in the life of the church.

Programs require leadership, places to do the programs, buy-in, and budgets. This is when things get technical and require logistical support. We need administrative systems and meetings where we plan and strategize. For some people, this is fun. For others, it can feel like they're being forced to watch a Senate committee meeting on C-SPAN. A snooze fest (at least for me). As a visionary I've learned to embrace the process, to enjoy taking an idea from its raw form to a full-fledged, legitimate program we can offer.

After bragging about how many people go to their church, the next thing on many lead pastor's boast about is what programs they offer. I've heard of amazing programs that churches offer, like a prom for severely handicapped children who wouldn't otherwise experience that moment or a business-men's luncheon that brings community leaders together. Some host the ever-reliable AA meetings or job training seminars. These programs become a selling point for many people searching for a church that meets a specific need.

You can even poll your neighbors to find out what they'd like to see offered in the community, then launch a program based on that feedback. Churches have gained a lot of goodwill, and grown, through these community-driven programs. There's nothing wrong with that—unless you start handing out gold medals to programs.

When programs become the main focus of your church, that's when it risks becoming a glorified community center run by social activists with inspi-rational posters and a Sunday service on the side. Programs bring in the funding, the attention, and the people. While that looks like success, I believe the church is called to be a living organism first, not a clunky institution with CEO's disguised as clergy.

When programs climb higher than third place on the priority list, the church can lose the soul of why it exists. Even worse, the Spirit of God may no longer distinguish them from any other nonprofit. Think about institutions like Harvard and Yale. They were once seminaries training up pastors and preachers for the pulpits across the globe. Now they're secularized bastions of academia, far removed from their Spirit-filled roots. Many churches today have followed that same trajectory.

Some of their programs are so well-recognized that they've attracted government grants. Sounds good on the surface but with funding often comes compromise. Instead of God being their source and provider, churches become reliant on secular economic sources. And as soon as you depend on a Babylonian system, your freedom to teach, preach, and eat what you want is regulated—and it's easy to bow to the immoral whims of your funding source.

You know where those compromises are resisted? In churches that put the presence of God first. They refuse to be bought off or enticed to shift their God-given mission for a more polished, more profitable program. These are the churches that say, "If it doesn't flow from His presence, we don't want it."

Program-first churches may have some success stories—they might even go viral with a good PR moment—but rarely do they produce the kind of long-term, mass transformation that comes from a true move of God. Take the YMCA or even some branches of the Salvation Army for example. Once birthed in revival, they now are largely operating as humanitarian organizations with little spiritual power. It's not that they're doing harm; it's just that they're not operating in the fullness of their original call.

God won't share His glory with the idols we make of our organizations no matter how well-meaning they are. God is patient. He'll wait for the right time, the right people, and the right posture. He'll back programs birthed from His heart, and those programs will carry generational impact.

Programs with God at the center, that care for and equip the people God wants us to reach are the ones He'll resource. It could look like a chicken sandwich joint reinvesting profits into employee development and faith-based initiatives. Being led by God doesn't mean we'll have janky systems and janky setups. We can still be excellent. But it does mean we don't chase paper and ask God to bless the idols we've made.

Remember Abraham? He got impatient. He wanted to help God get the promise moving and ended up with Ishmael. Ishmael was Abraham's flesh interfering with God's perfect timing. Many church programs are Ishmaels—impressive but not God's promised best. Now imagine how many generations were impacted by that one misstep. How many churches have birthed "Ishmael" programs that appeared successful on the surface, yet spiritually gave rise to confusion and opposition to the very "Isaac" programs God intended to bless? What looked like blessing was really a substitute— an Ishmael born out of impatience, not promise. In chasing results, we sometimes produce ministries that become antagonistic to the move of God we were actually called to reproduce.

Programs in their proper place—bronze medal spot—will bless people for generations and glorify God, who entrusted them to us. They help people find hope, resources, and healing within the church instead of having to go outside the community to get help. That's when programs serve their true purpose: meeting real needs while being fueled by real power.

So, let's build the programs. Let's have the strategic meetings. Let's serve people with excellence. But let's never forget: gold belongs to God, silver to His people, and bronze to the programs we build to serve them both.

Round 4 | Down for the Count

There's a reason tourists still line up to visit historic Catholic churches. The awe-inspiring cathedrals with their towering ceilings, ornate carvings, and vivid stained-glass windows were designed not just to impress but to express. These structures were built as sacred spaces meant to reflect the majesty of God. Every detail, from the spires that reach toward heaven to the gold-plated chalices and the aroma of burning incense, points to the divine. The stained glass isn't just decoration. It is theology in light, illuminating Scripture for the illiterate masses. The architecture is worship in stone.

Say what you want about their theology, Catholics understand something powerful: *space matters.* A sacred space can preach without words. The aesthetics of property—the excellence of how a building looks and feels—communicates a message. When people come to hear about the wonder of who God is and what He can do, the environment should reflect that excellence, not contradict it.

Our gatherings should take place in spaces that reflect the collective generosity and stewardship of God's people. They should not be opulent for opulence's sake, but they should honor God by being clean, well maintained, beautiful spaces that say, "This matters to us because He matters to us."

Look at how God instructed Moses to construct the Tabernacle. Every pole, every covering, every bowl and candle was intentional. God didn't wing it. He gave Moses exact specifications for the dimensions and materials and even the recipe for the anointing oil. Gold wasn't reserved for kings; it was used for the holy things. The Tabernacle wasn't just functional; it was prophetic. Every element represented something heavenly.

And check out what happened when the tribes of Israel encamped around that mobile sanctuary. The order, the positioning, the layout—all of it created such divine alignment that even the pagan prophet Balaam, hired to curse them, could only bless them. The presence of God in the center brought harmony to the whole.

Then Solomon took things to another level when he turned the Tabernacle into a permanent temple. Using his wisdom and wealth, he constructed one of the most magnificent buildings ever created. The Queen of Sheba didn't just marvel at his riches. She was stunned into silence by the splendor of the Temple. That's what honoring God with your property can look like.

If property is so significant then, why does it come last on the list of priorities?

Because while it can be helpful to people, it doesn't impress God the way we think it does. He's not opposed to beautiful spaces, but He values souls more than stones, obedience more than opulence. Property is a tool, not a trophy.

When churches put property first—or even second or third—they drift toward idolatry. God said, "You shall have no other gods before Me" (Exodus 20:3). But some ministries have made buildings their god. Maybe that's why God allowed the Temple to be ransacked. The people treated the building as their security instead of the One the building was made to honor.

Today, a fancy facility can give the illusion of success. Grand sanctuaries filled with aging congregants who shuffle through like museum curators, reminiscing about what God *used* to do there. No new movement. No fresh fire. Just polished pews and perfect HVAC systems. When property becomes an idol, apprehension begins to grip the lead pastor's heart. It shows up subtly at first—a hesitancy to speak truth too boldly for fear of offending the high-dollar donors who help keep the lights on. There's a quiet pressure to keep things comfortable, especially when changes or updates need to be made to the aging facility. Suddenly, the fear of losing a contributor outweighs the fear of losing God's presence. Decisions about design, direction, and decor become more about who might leave than who might be reached.

This is when the church starts to prioritize relics over relevance. Leadership—or more often the power players behind the scenes—begin to care more about preserving the status quo than pioneering what could reach the next generation. What once was a place of movement and ministry becomes a monument to memories. The building starts to feel like a museum filled with yesterday's stories instead of a launching pad for today's miracles. Property is meant to serve the mission, not steer it. When the church starts protecting property more than pursuing people, we've got our priorities out of order.

Property should serve the presence, the people, and the programs not the other way around.

I've seen once-thriving churches sold and turned into bars, restaurants, or community centers. Some have even become mosques. Once they lit up neighborhoods with God's glory, now they serve cocktails or host dance parties. Why? Because the property became the point, and the people inside stopped transforming the streets outside.

Evangelists get this. I can hear them shouting, "Amen!" as they read. For them, property is simply an address to gather the lost or a launchpad to send the found. It's a base of operations, not the mission itself. If our greatest ambition is to be holy property managers, we're wasting the tremendous opportunity to steward spaces that inspire faith for years to come. If the most powerful thing happening in your ministry is your electrical panel, you're in trouble.

So why then is property an honorable mention? Because in sports, that phrase means you did something worth noting but not something worth a medal. That's exactly the place property holds. It's worth noting. It matters. But it's not the prize.

Let property be honorable. Let it be excellent. But let it always be the servant not the master of God, God's people, and God's purpose.

When we honor God with our spaces—but don't idolize them—we build something that can bless generations. Buildings will come and go. But what we do in them—what God does through us in them—is what leaves a legacy.

Conclusion |
Undisputed Champion

The ark of the covenant, which we talked about at the start of this section, had two seraphim (special angels) crafted on its lid. That whole lid—the mercy seat—was made of pure gold. Gold is one of the most fascinating and valuable metals on the planet. It's malleable yet strong. It conducts heat and electricity. It doesn't corrode. It's safe enough to place in our mouths and strong enough to hold its place in our teeth. It's beautiful, practical, and enduring—just like God's presence should be among us.

But here's the hard truth: while God called us to carry the gold of His presence, we've often settled for golden calves. The Israelites didn't achieve true freedom when they built the calf; they just got enslaved to another master. And we've done the same. We've crafted our own golden calves in the form of worship experiences that move emotions but lack the substance of God. We've exalted personalities and platforms—preachers with sneakers, viral sermons, celebrity pastors—over presence. We've even turned our pain into an idol. Church hurt elevated to a place that God never intended it to occupy.

Golden calves are anything we shape in our image of God, but without His breath. They're the things we get a "holy cow" over when someone challenges or changes them. And the truth is, there's a lot of stuff competing to win the gold in our hearts.

But here's my warrior cry: Let's reprioritize. Let's re-center. Let's return. The presence of God must win the gold every time we gather—whether it's in a sanctuary, a storefront, a house, or a coffee shop. Wherever we come together to hear from God, those places must become houses of prayer, resting places for His glory. Because if we get this priority right, if His presence is our first pursuit, everything else will follow.

God is jealous for our love, and we should be jealous for His. I won't pretend this path is easy or even popular, but if you're reading this and something in you is burning with a holy frustration, if you're tired of church as usual and hungry for the real thing, you're not alone.

And maybe, just maybe, if this book goes viral, it won't be because it's catchy or clever—it'll be a sign.

A signal that the tide is turning. That the atmosphere is shifting. That a righteous remnant—those who haven't bowed their knee to compromise and who are done kissing idols—is rising.

So rise up. Fight with me. Let's become champions who contend for a golden era of the presence of God, the fame of Jesus, and the wonders of His Holy Spirit. Let that be our magnus opus—our great work, our ultimate offering.

Let's fight for God to win gold.

About the Author

Jamie Centeno leads a thriving inner-city movement called In The Light in the city of Philadelphia. It's there where, as a second-generation pastor, he carries himself as the chief innovation officer (CIO). He is passionate to build the body of Christ to be the spiritual powerhouse it's meant to be while beautifying this bride of Christ for generations, denominations and nations to be inspired to do the same. He has authored three books: *Heavolution*, *RelationShift*, and *Milk & Honey*.